Sous Vide

Getting Started With Vacuum-Sealed Cooking (Authoritative Guide, Perfectly Cooked, Easy Gourmet At Home)

Sarah P. Williamson

Sous Vide: Getting Started With Vacuum-Sealed Cooking (Authoritative Guide, Perfectly Cooked, Easy Gourmet At Home)

Table of Contents

1 - Introduction

I want to thank you and congratulate you for buying this book, "Sous Vide Book One: Getting Started with Vacuum-Sealed Cooking".

Sous vide cooking is a simple and foolproof technique that ensures that you get tastier and more nutritious food. Even better, once you've gotten the process down, you are assured of getting the same great results every time you cook.

This book will teach you all the techniques you need to know in order to successfully cook sous vide, even without any fancy gadgets. We also provide you with a selection of recipes that you can try out once you've started cooking sous vide, so you can treat your family to some great dishes.

Thanks again for buying this book, I hope you enjoy it!

2 - What is Sous Vide?

Sous vide is French for "under vacuum" and refers to a culinary technique in which food is vacuum sealed and cooked while submerged in water that has been heated to a very precise and consistent temperature. Once the food hits the desired cooking temperature or time, it is taken out and served. Although it can be used to cook a variety of food, sous vide is most useful in cooking seafood and meat.

In conventional methods, food has to be cooked at a temperature high enough that its internal temperature reaches the level required to cook it. However, the risk is that the food would become overcooked when left at this temperature too long, turning it dry or burning it. Conversely, if the food is taken from the heat too early, the center may still be raw even if the outside is already cooked.

Sous vide addresses this problem by immersing the food in a water bath where the temperature of the water is set at the exact temperature required to ensure that its internal temperature reaches cooking level. This means that even if you leave the food immersed for a longer time than absolutely necessary, it does not overcook since its internal temperature cannot exceed the water temperature.

Sous vide had previously been mainly practiced by professional chefs since the equipment needed was expensive. In recent years, however, the prices have gone down, allowing home cooks to start trying sous vide cooking at home.

History of Sous Vide

The basic idea of cooking food packaged in airtight containers was actually first conceived in the eighteenth century by inventor Sir Benjamin Thompson, although the heat transfer medium was air rather than water. But it was never more than a theory to him, and Thompson never developed a dedicated machine to put his ideas to practical use.

However, the basic idea was later developed as a method of food preservation, with food being vacuum-sealed in jars, and then boiled to kill harmful bacteria and other contaminants like yeasts. As long as the seal remained unbroken, the food inside would remain unspoiled.

In the 1960s, cryovacking or vacuum sealing food under pressure in food-grade plastic pouches and film was developed. This paved the way for modern sous vide.

In 1974, Chef George Pralus, who was working at the Michelin three-star rated La Maison Troisgros, was looking for a method of cooking delicate fois gras that reduced wastage. When fois gras was cooked using traditional methods, it shrank to nearly half its size, which cost the restaurant a lot of money.

Pralus had heard about the vacuum-packing method being used to preserve foods so he decided to try applying it to food preparation. He wrapped the fois gras in multiple layers of plastic to create a vacuum and then submerged it in a water bath to cook it. The experiment was successful and sous vide, as we know it today, was born.

While Pralus was developing sous vide as a cooking technique, Bruno Goussalt was experimenting with it as a way of preserving food on a large scale. His experiments paved the way for sous vide companies that made classical dishes for restaurants that only needed to be reheated to serve.

Since Goussalt's methods focused on food preservation, they paved the way for sous vide to be used professionally since they allowed it to meet French standards for food safety.

However, sous vide was initially mainly used by professional chefs over the next few decades. This method of cooking was still considered mostly experimental and potentially dangerous if not done properly. Also, the equipment used for sous vide cooking was made for commercial kitchens, costing thousands of dollars, and thus was too expensive for most households.

But in the 2000s, books about sous vide, such as chef Thomas Keller's Under Pressure: Cooking Sous Vide, were becoming popular, sparking interest in technique among serious home chefs.

Since affordable equipment was not available to them, they experimented with homemade kits using sealable bags and kettles. Although these were successful to some degree, it was only when smaller sous vide equipment specifically designed for home use began being produced that the technique really achieved its current popularity.

Basic Features of Sous Vide Cooking

The food to be cooked is vacuum-sealed in a plastic bag. This seals in the aroma and juices of the food that may be lost during the cooking process.

The bag is immersed in a water bath that is heated to the exact cooking temperature. This ensures the food cannot be overcooked since the temperature of the food cannot exceed that of the water in the bath. In traditional cooking methods, the temperature must be set higher than the final desired cook temperature and the food must be removed from the heat to avoid overcooking.

The vacuum inside the bag allows the cooked food to be stored for a longer period of time as long as it is placed immediately in the refrigerator while still sealed.

You no longer need to time your cooking so precisely. In traditional cooking methods, food is cooked at a high temperature that fluctuates, so you have to time it precisely. If you leave the food on the flame for just a few minutes too long, the food may be overcooked or not taste as good.

On the other hand, with sous vide, there is a higher margin of error; even if you overcook for just a few minutes, the food will still taste as good.

Benefits of Sous Vide Cooking

Since sous vide allows you to cook food for longer periods at lower temperatures, it allows you to enjoy many benefits, including:

Tastier food since sous-vide cooking means it does not lose its original aroma, flavor, weight and natural color since it cooks at a lower temperature. Food also does not lose its form or dehydrate while cooking.

Since food cooked sous-vide maintains enhanced flavor, you don't need additional fat or salt to taste; the food also retains its nutrients while cooking.

You can get more consistent results when you cook since precise temperatures are used during cooking.

You have more control over the timing of your cooking. By setting the water bath at the right temperature, you can cook the food more slowly so that it will be ready by the time you get home. You can even set it to cook overnight so that it will be done when you get up in the morning.

Cooking meals sous-vide is quick and easy. Once you've prepared the food, all you have to do is place it in the pre-heated water bath. You can be done in as little as thirty minutes.

You can place individual servings in their own bags, allowing you to easily cook large quantities for dinner parties and other get-togethers.

Since you can cook smaller portions, there is less food wastage, saving you money. Many sous vide water baths also use less energy than traditional electric or gas ovens.

Food cooked sous vide lasts longer. You can prepare food in advance, then freeze it after cooling, and thaw it for later.

3 - Sous Vide Equipment: What You Need

One of the best things about sous vide cooking is that you can choose your equipment based on your budget. If you have the money to spend, you can buy sous vide water baths with temperature controls.

But if you are just starting out and have limited funds, you can buy a more affordable immersion circulator that ensures heat is evenly distributed throughout the water but does not have its own dedicated water container.

Although specialized sous vide machines are more expensive, they allow you to start cooking at once and are basically foolproof; all you have to do is fill the container with water, set the temperature and place the bags with the food you're cooking into the bath. In addition, these machines generate higher temperatures and are insulated to ensure that the cooking temperature remains at an even level.

When choosing one of these machines, one of the main considerations is the capacity of the water bath. Generally, the machines available have capacities that range from a low of five liters to as much as 120 liters.

A machine with a larger capacity gives you more flexibility to cook the quantities that you need, but of course will be bulkier and more difficult to store if you have limited counter space. Also, when deciding on the capacity, keep in mind that you should fill only half the bath with pouches since there needs to be room to allow the water to circulate.

Other considerations to keep in mind are their ability to keep the temperature stable and its heating power, which determines how long it takes to reach the required temperature. Some models also come with a vacuum sealer that makes it more convenient to use since you can easily ensure that there is no air in the bag before you place it in the water bath.

Immersion circulators are essentially heating wands that are placed into a water container; they will heat the water and keep it at a consistent temperature. They can heat up to five gallons of water, providing you with plenty of flexibility for cooking.

The main disadvantage of using these machines is that, since they are used in open containers, there are issues with water evaporation and heat loss. But you can address this issue by using a polycarbonate container with a lid and then cutting a hole in the lid to accommodate the circulator. An inexpensive plastic cooler also works very well since it is insulated which will help maintain the temperature.

Alternately, you can cover the opening of the container with aluminum foil or plastic wrap to keep the heat in and reduce evaporation. However, they are not easy to remove and replace, which makes it difficult if you want to add water or adjust the food pouches.

The simplest and most effective solution, however, is to simply place Ping-Pong balls on top of the bath. A layer of these balls will condense steam so it drips back down and helps maintain the water level while keeping the water insulated. You can also easily place and remove food packets from the water bath and the balls will adjust to the shape of your water container; the balls are also reusable.

If you don't have the budget to purchase a circulator or stand-alone sous vide machine, however, it is possible to create a basic sous vide setup at home using basic materials such as a pot and a stove; however, you will need to invest in an instant-read digital thermometer if you don't have one. We will describe how in the following chapter.

4 - How to Cook Sous Vide

To give you a better understanding of how to cook sous-vide, here is a step-by-step overview of the process.

Determine the right temperature for the food you are planning to cook. This is one of the essential steps in cooking sous vide since the temperature of the water has to be as close as possible to the optimal temperature to get the best results.

For beginners, however, you can start by determining the temperature range for the 'done-ness' of the food you are cooking, i.e. medium-rare, medium, traditional, as well as the type of food, i.e. chicken or beef.

Preparing the food for cooking

There are a number of ways to prepare food before placing it in the bag, ranging from pre-portioning, slicing, blanching and smoking.

Package the food. Basically, this involves sealing the food to be cooked in plastic bags that you can remove the air from, such as food grade Ziploc bags. For some foods, however, glass jars can be an option.

Cook the food at the required time. Although sous vide is generally used for cooking, you can also use it to tenderize tough pieces of meat. Tenderizing means you will have to cook the meat for hours or even days, depending on how tender you want it to be.

Also, a consideration when deciding cooking times is food safety. Since the temperatures used in sous-vide are relatively low, you can only cook food for a limited amount of time. This range is from 40-degrees F to 140-degrees F, and food cooked at this temperature for longer than a few hours becomes unsafe.

Also, a consideration is the size of the piece you are cooking; if the piece is too big, the heat may not be enough to ensure that it is thoroughly cooked, leaving certain areas vulnerable to microbial spoilage.

Adding finishing touches

Since the temperatures used in sous vide cooking are too low to brown meat, you have to sear steaks after cooking to give them a crust and the expected flavor. However, you can sear meat before and after cooking to get better results.

5 - Basic Sous Vide Cooking

Before you invest in sous vide equipment, you might want to try cooking using the sous vide method first, so you can see how it works and what food cooked with this technique tastes like.

The basic method simply involves bagging some strips of food in a Ziploc bag and immersing them in hot water. Here are two simple recipes you can try; all you need is a deep kitchen sink that can accommodate several gallons of hot water or a five-gallon cooler that will keep in the heat.

The first recipe is for cooking salmon filet. This delicate fish is ideal to cook sous vide since it easily contracts and dries out when exposed to too much heat. Take some salmon strips and place one or more strips per bag, but make sure that they are in a single layer. Make sure that you remove most of the air (use the water displacement method described later in the chapter).

Add some olive oil or melted butter, and then fill your container with hot water that is around 122-degrees F; if you use your kitchen sink, you don't need to worry about excessive heat loss since large volumes of hot water will be able to retain its temperature. Immerse the bags in water for around fifteen minutes. Then remove the salmon from the water.

Once you've finished cooking the salmon, you can finish it before serving by searing it in a pan. First heat the pan until it is sizzling; test it by flicking some water drops onto it. Place a thin layer of oil on the pan (olive oil if you have it, otherwise canola oil will do). Place the filets on the pan with the skin side down, and let brown for thirty seconds to one minute.

You can also use this basic method for cooking steaks. Take a pair of strip steaks (less than ¼-inch) and season them. Bag them in a single layer, and then add some canola oil. Boil some water in a pot until it reaches 145-degrees F.

Fill the cooler or kitchen sink with water and immerse the bags; make sure they are completely immersed to ensure they will be fully cooked. Allow the steaks to cook for around an hour. Then remove from the water and serve as desired or finish by heating in a pan.

Since cooking times are more forgiving with sous vide, you

don't have to worry about overcooking even if you leave the food in the hot water for longer than the recommended cooking time; just don't take them out too early since they may be under-cooked.

As we mentioned in the previous chapter, you can create a basic sous vide setup without having to invest in a standalone machine or immersion circulator. All you need is a pot and a digital instant-read thermometer. The biggest challenge with using this basic setup is maintaining the required cooking temperature long enough to cook the food.

Since pots can easily lose temperature through the sides, as well as through water evaporation, you will have to constantly adjust the heat on the stove to ensure that the temperature remains steady. Fortunately, you don't have to keep the temperature at an exact level, and losing a degree or two is not that big of a deal.

All you have to do to cook sous vide is to fill the pot with water up to a level that it will not overflow once you place the food bags inside. Then heat the water until it reaches the required temperature, using the digital thermometer to measure it.

This can take a bit of time and practice to get right; however, frequently stirring the water can help it reach the required temperature more quickly. To help you monitor the temperature, you can attach the digital thermometer on a binder clip or a skewer so you can mount it to the side of the pot.

Choosing Cooking Times and Temperatures

When you cook a piece of meat using traditional methods, one of the major issues you have to address is that the outside heats more quickly than the center. Thus, it becomes difficult to determine when the meat is completely done; a lot of times, the outside is already done while the center is still relatively uncooked.

With sous vide cooking, however, this discrepancy is easily addressed, allowing you to get a perfectly cooked piece of meat. Since you are cooking using a precise temperature that is maintained at a static level, you can more readily predict how long it will take the center to reach cooking temperature.

Once submerged in the water bath, the food will cook evenly all over, from edge to center, because the cooking temperature and the external temperatures are one and the same.

When determining how long to cook meat, the main consideration is the thickness of the meat; the thicker the meat, the longer it takes to cook. In addition, although sous vide is more forgiving when it comes to cooking times, there is still a maximum time beyond which you should not keep food in the water, otherwise it becomes mushy.

6 - Guide to choosing the right temperatures and times for cooking various food groups

Fish

Fish are cooked only for a short time and the result is moist and flaky. You can eat it as is with some lemon juice or olive oil or with a fresh vegetable salsa as a side dish, make it a sandwich or add it to traditional dishes such as fish chowder and fish stew.

Generally, depending on the level of doneness you want, fish is cooked at 104-degrees F (rare sushi); 122-degrees F (medium rare sushi); 132-degrees F (medium rare) and 140-degrees F (medium) for 10 to 30 minutes. For most cuts, however, setting your machine to 130-degrees F will be sufficient.

Chicken

Sous vide results in chicken that is very moist and uniformly tender, making it the ideal basis for dishes that use chicken with a coating, such as fried chicken and chicken parmigiana.

Generally, the chicken should be cooked at 147-degrees F for one to four hours (breast) and 4 to 8 hours (thighs or legs). Although you can cook chicken at less than 140-degrees F, it tastes raw.

Eggs can be cooked at a range of 135-degrees F (safe to eat but is 'raw') to 158-degrees F (very hard boiled), with the ideal at 148-degrees F, although you can experiment to find the right temperature. Some people may boil it for two to five minutes after cooking to solidify the egg while without overcooking the yolk.

Pork

Sous vide allows you to cook pork medium-rare while maintaining food safety, as well as tenderizing tougher cuts by cooking them for longer at temperatures low enough to avoid drying them out. According to FDA guidelines, pork is safe when cooked at 130-degrees F for more than 112 minutes and 140-degrees F for over 12 minutes.

Generally, when cooking pork you can set your machine to 131-degrees F (medium rare) for six to twelve hours or 140-degrees F (medium) for five to ten hours. For tougher cuts you can cook it at 155-degrees F: to get it well done. You can also cook frozen pork chops without having to defrost them first; just add an additional fifteen to twenty minutes cooking time. Cooking times for various cuts are as follows:

- Tenderloin: medium rare 3 to 6 hours/medium 2 to 4 hours

- Pork loin chop: medium rare 3 to 5 hours/medium 2 to 4 hours

- Pork loin roast: medium rare 4 to 8 hours/medium 4 to 6 hours

- Pork ribs chop/roast: medium rare 5 to 8 hours/medium 4 to 7 hours

- Pork sirloin chop/roast: medium rare 6 to 12 hours/medium 5 to 10 hours/well done 10 to 16 hours (roast)

- Ribs Back/Baby Back/Country Style: medium rare 8 to 12 hours/medium 8 to 12 hours/well 12 to 24 hours

- Spare Ribs: medium rare/rare/well 12 to 24 hours

- Fresh Ham (Pork Leg): medium rare/rare/well 10 to 20 hours

- Ground Pork: medium rare/rare 2 to 4 hours

- Pork Sausage: medium rare/rare/well 2 to 3 hours

- Pork Chops: medium rare 3 to 6 hours/medium 2 to 4 hours

- Pork Belly/Fresh Side: low 140-degrees F 2 to 3 days/in-between 160-degrees F 18 to 36 hours/high 180-degrees F 12 to 18 hours

Beef Roasts

Cooking tough cuts of beef sous vide allows you to tenderize them without drying them out since they never go beyond medium rare cooking temperatures. Generally, you can set your machine to 131-degrees F to 140-degrees F for most cuts, although you can set it to 160-degrees F if you want them to be well done. Cooking times are as follows:

- Prime Rib/ Sirloin/Tri-Tip Roast: medium rare/medium 5 to 10 hours

- Chuck Roast/Short Ribs: medium rare/medium 2 to 3 days, well 1 to 2 days

- Top Round Roast: medium rare/medium 1 to 3 days, well 1 to 2 days

- Bottom Round Roast/Brisket/Cheek/Shank/Pot Roast: medium rare/medium 2 to 3 days, well 1 to 2 days

- Beef Stew: medium rare/medium 4 to 8 hours

Beef Steaks

More tender cuts of beef are cooked at 131-degrees F to 140-degrees F and should not exceed this temperature since the beef will begin to dry out. Cooking times are generally between 2 to 4 hours, resulting in a more tender steak. You can cook tougher steaks for longer times, and they will be as tender as tenderloin.

Cooking times are:

- Tenderloin/Porterhouse/T-Bone/Top Loin Strip: medium rare/medium 2 to 3 hours

- Ribeye/Rib: medium rare/medium 2 to 8 hours

- Tri-Tip/Sirloin: medium rare/medium 2 to 10 hours

- Flat Iron/Shoulder/Blade: medium rare/medium 4 to 10 hours

- Chuck/Eye Round/Top Round/Skirt/Flank: medium rare/medium 1 to 2 days

- Hamburger: medium rare/medium 2 to 4 hours

Turkey

Cooking turkey sous vide results in meat that is very moist and uniformly tender. Generally, turkey should be cooked at temperatures above 140-degrees F, with the ideal cooking temperature at 136-degrees F (rare) or 147-degrees F (medium) at 1 to 4 hours for breasts and 148-degrees F (ideal) for 4 to 8 hours for thighs, drumsticks, and legs; if you want the latter at medium-rare doneness, cook the latter at 140-degrees F for 3 to 4 hours and at 160-degrees F for 18 to 24 hours if they are going to be shredded. You can also use the juices in the bag as gravy to serve the turkey with.

However, you should remove the skin before cooking because it will not become crisp; you can crisp it before serving by frying it in a skillet with a little oil or bake it in the oven at 375-degrees F on a baking sheet with raised edges to catch the fat.

Duck

Cooking duck sous vide allows you to consistently get outstanding results but also easily confit duck. Duck is generally cooked at 131-degrees F to medium rate doneness and for 2 to 4 hours. If you are planning to cook duck for shredding, you should cook it at 176-degrees F to well doneness and for 8 to 10 hours; the duck will still be moist but will be fall apart ready for shredding. To make duck confit, all you have to do is prepare the meat by curing it and then bag it with some duck fat; cook for 10 to 20 hours at 167-degrees F.

As with other poultry meats such as chicken and turkey, you should remove the skin before putting it in the bag and crisp it separately.

Shellfish

Cooking this seafood sous vide lets you avoid the pitfalls of cooking it the traditional way, which is that it becomes tough, and gives you very tender results. Although the ideal cooking temperature is 132-degrees F, shellfish will not be pasteurized and you should avoid it if you have a susceptible immune system or the shellfish is sushi-grade.

Cooking times and temperatures are as follows:

- Lobster: cooking time 15 to 40 minutes medium rare 126-degrees F/medium 140-degrees F

- Shrimp: cooking time 15 to 35 minutes medium rare (sushi) 122-degrees F/medium rare 132-degrees F

- Squid: pre-sear 45 minutes to 1 hour at 113-degrees F/low heat 2 to 4 hours at 138-degrees F/high heat 60 minutes at 180-degrees F

- Soft shell crab: 3 hours at 145-degrees F to 150-degrees F

- Scallops: pre-sear 15 to 35 minutes at 122-degrees F

- Octopus: slow 4 to 7 hours at 170-degrees F/fast 2 to 3 hours at 180-degrees F

Lamb

Sous vide is the perfect method for cooking this meat due to its toughness. By cooking it at lower temperatures for a longer period, you can tenderize the meat without drying it out. Tough cuts of lamb are generally cooked for one to two days to fully tenderize although tenderer roasts will be fully tenderized at 2 to 4 hours.

Lamb is generally cooked for 2 to 3 hours at 131-degrees F to get medium-rare doneness, for 1 to 3 hours at 140-degrees F to get medium doneness or for 1 to 2 hours at 126-degrees F to get rare doneness. However, you should exercise care since lamb cooked at less than 130-degrees F is still not pasteurized and may not be safe to eat if you have a sensitive immune system.

Cooking instructions for lamb:

- Lamb leg, boneless: cooking time 18 to 36 hours medium rare at 131-degrees F/medium at 140-degrees F

- Lamb leg, bone-in: medium rare 2 to 3 days at 131-degrees F/medium 1 to 3 days at 140-degrees F

- Shank/Shoulder: medium rare 1 to 2 days at 131-degrees F/medium 1 to 2 days at 140-degrees F/well 165-degrees F 18 to 36 hours (shoulder) 1 to 2 days (shank)

- Breast: cooking time 20 to 28 hours medium-rare 131-degrees F/medium 140-degrees F/well 165-degrees F

- Ribs: cooking time 22 to 26 hours medium-rare 131-degrees F/medium 140-degrees F/well 165-degrees F

- Osso Buco: cooking time 1 to 2 days medium-rare 131-degrees F/medium 140-degrees F/well 165-degrees F

Fruits and vegetables

By cooking these foods sous vide you can preserve their nutrients and tenderize them without risking them becoming too soft and losing their structure. In addition, any nutrients that drip out of vegetables will be caught in the bag so they can be reused.

When cooking fruits and vegetables sous vide, set the machine to 183-degrees F. Cooking times will vary depending on their firmness. The cooking times for selected fruits and vegetables are:

- Broccoli: 20 to 30 minutes

- Brussels Sprouts: 45 to 60 minutes

- Cabbage: 30 to 45 minutes

- Cauliflower: 20 to 30 minutes/puree 2 hours

- Zucchini: 30 to 60 minutes

- Pumpkin: 45 to 60 minutes

- Leek: 30 to 60 minutes

- Onion: 35 to 45 minutes

6 - GUIDE TO CHOOSING THE RIGHT TEMPERATURES AND TIMES FOR COOKING VARIOUS FOOD GROUPS

- Green Beans: 30 to 45 minutes

- Corn: 30 to 45 minutes

- Pea Pods: 30 to 40 minutes

- Beet: 30 minutes to 1 hour

- Carrot: 40 minutes to 1 hour

- Turnip: 30 to 45 minutes

- Potatoes: small 30 minutes to 1 hour/large 1 to 2 hours

- Sweet potatoes: small 45 minutes to 1 hour/large 1 hour to 90 minutes

- Artichokes: 45 to 75 minutes

- Asparagus: 30 to 40 minutes

- Apple: 25 to 40 minutes

- Pears: 25 to 35 minutes

6 - GUIDE TO CHOOSING THE RIGHT TEMPERATURES AND TIMES FOR COOKING VARIOUS FOOD GROUPS

- Banana: 10 to 15 minutes

- Cherries: 15 to 25 minutes

- Pineapple: 45 minutes to 1 hour

- Plums: 15 to 20 minutes

- Peaches: 30 minutes to 1 hour

- Eggplant: 30 to 45 minutes

- Garlic: 1 hour to 90 minutes

7 - Preparing Food for Sous Vide Cooking

The basic way to prepare food for sous vide is to slice or pre-portion it. This is recommended for delicate cuts of meat and fish since it would lessen the cooking time and ensure that the food does not become mushy.

Smaller portions mean the center of the meat or fish reaches final cooking temperature more quickly. It also ensures food safety since every part of the piece reaches cooking temperature. However, tougher cuts of meat can be cooked in larger pieces since you get better results with longer cooking times.

Searing meat

If you are cooking steak and other meats, they will not achieve the crispy and flavorful skin that gives them most of their flavor when cooking sous vide due to the low temperatures used. Hence, meat has to be seared before cooking, although there are some who prefer to do it afterward.

Searing beforehand has several benefits, including reducing the chances of overcooking and ensuring better flavor since the flavor compounds penetrate the meat during cooking. In addition, you ensure better food safety since pre-searing kills most of the germs that can cause the meat to go bad.

However, the crust will be softened during the cooking process, and to restore it, you will have to sear the meat again before serving. But pre-searing means the process will be quicker.

In addition, pre-searing is not recommended for the meat of lamb and other grass-fed animals, since it can result in unpleasant flavors when cooking sous vide for a long time.

Before searing meat, you will have to dry it out since a moist surface will prevent browning, forcing you to cook it for longer and risking overcooking. Once you take it out of the packet, pat it dry with clean towels or paper towels.

Dry it a few minutes before searing so that the meat will cool slightly and any moisture left behind will evaporate. However, if you would like to get a deeper crust, you can cool the meat for longer, since this will give you more time to brown it before you risk overcooking.

There are a number of ways you can sear meat. The easiest

method is to sear it in a pan, which is particularly effective if you have a cast-iron skillet; if you are planning to sear fish or other delicate seafood, however, a stainless steel pan should be used.

All you have to do is place a thin layer of refined oil with a high smoke point (i.e. canola oil) on the skillet and heat it over medium or high heat until it starts to smoke and turns brown, and then cook the food for 45 to 90 seconds per side until it browns.

Alternately, you can deep fry food to brown it. Use a pan filled with oil just below the halfway level that has been heated to 375-degrees – 400-degrees F. Place the food in the oil and fry for 30 to 90 seconds.

For roasts, you can use an oven. Coat the roast with your desired coating after sous vide cooking, and then cook it in an oven set to 500-degrees F. You can also use a grill, whether gas-fired or coal.

Make sure the heat is turned all the way up or the coals are as hot as possible and let the bars fully heat after closing the lid. Brush the meat with some oil and place on the grill with the lid open; cook for 45 to 90 seconds, until grill marks form and the meat is browned.

Finally, you can use a torch, which is particularly effective for foods that have an uneven surface. If you are planning to invest in a torch for searing, you will have to buy a larger one that is suited for industrial uses such as light welding and soldering copper, and which produces temperatures of more than 3500-degrees F, which is enough to sear food in 2 to 3 minutes.

Although there are a wide variety of torches available on the market, the most reliable ones seem to be those produced by BernzOmatic, which has been in existence for over a century.

The most affordable torches are those that use propane gas, although some may prefer MAP-Pro, even though it carries a price premium. When searing, make sure that the torch is producing the fully oxidizing flame, which is dark blue, relatively short and produces a hissing sound.

If you sear food using a large yellow flame, you may end up producing food with 'torch taste', which is unpleasant. Point the torch at the food and make sure to keep it moving to avoid uneven browning.

Blanching vegetables

You can cook vegetables sous vide by placing entire pieces into the bag and then slicing them after they're done. However, you should blanch them before cooking to preserve their texture and color. Simply immerse the vegetables in boiling water for two seconds to destroy the enzymes that cause browning.

Seasoning food

If you would like to add dry or wet condiments to food before cooking, use smaller quantities than you would normally since the flavors will be more intense. You will also have to vacuum pack the food.

To ensure that liquid condiments are not sucked into the machine when vacuum packing, freeze them beforehand; however, this will not be necessary if you are using a vacuum chamber since it can handle liquids easily.

Sealing Food for Sous Vide

When sealing food inside the bag for sous vide, you don't actually need to create a vacuum seal for the process to work; you only need to make sure that most of the air inside the bag is removed. This ensures that flavors are sealed in and not lost to the water; bags that have air in them also float, which means that some of the food may not be cooked since it is out of the water.

The most common containers used to package food for sous vide cooking are sealable plastic bags. Use food-grade polyethylene, polypropylene or low-density polyethylene bags.

You can use specially made sous vide bags or high-quality Ziploc bags (gallon freezer bags will be big enough to accommodate several servings at once). However, if you're planning to cook food above 158-degrees F, you should use sous vide bags rather than Ziploc bags, since the seams of the latter may fail; if you don't have any sous vide bags, you can improvise by double bagging Ziploc bags.

Vacuum sealers are not necessary to cook sous vide since the seals of Ziploc or sous vide bags are secure enough.

However, if you plan to cook a lot of vegetables, you might want to invest in an inexpensive sealer in order to be assured of the best results. You can also use the sealer to store food so that they will keep longer by removing the air inside the bag.

Even without a vacuum sealer, however, there is a simple way to ensure that air is removed from your sous vide bags.

1. Fill a bowl or your kitchen sink with water.

2. Place ingredients in Ziploc bag up to an inch from the mouth, then close the seal with only a small opening left.

3. Slowly submerge the bag in the water until the open mouth is left exposed. This will force all the air out.

4. Zip the opening closed.

What about canning jars as an alternative? Some people prefer glass jars for sous vide due to concerns about the safety of plastic, even though Ziploc bags are perfectly safe since they only soften at 195-degrees F that is lower than most temperatures used in sous vide. Although they work fine, it will take longer for your food to cook.

In addition, when cooking meat you will have to cover it with a cooking liquid such as oil to ensure that it is cooked safely. However, jars are recommended if you are batch-cooking yogurt, custard or other foods that need to set; you can distribute portions among the small jars and then cook them.

8 - Tips for Successful Sous Vide Cooking

Don't let the water in the bath evaporate

If the water level falls below the heating coils of the sous vide machine or circulator motor, it can cause damage to the unit you are using. This is a particular issue if you are cooking for an extended period of time. So make sure that your water bath is covered with a lid, plastic wrap or layer of Ping-Pong balls.

Choose the seasonings and herbs you use carefully

Fresh herbs such as onions and garlic don't seem to do as well during sous vide cooking as dried ones such as black pepper and cumin. If left too long, these herbs may even overpower the flavor of the food and even eventually taste rancid.

Make sure that the bags are completely immersed in the hot water

If you have successfully removed all the air from the bag,

this should not be a problem unless the food item you are cooking is lightweight. In this case, you can add a food-safe weight to the bag, such as a stainless steel dull butter knife, a clean glass marble or other stainless steel items. To avoid contamination, put these in their own smaller pouch before placing them in the food bag.

If the issue is that the bags are moving up and down because of the immersion circulator's motor, you can help keep the bags in place by using binder clips to attach them to the side of the water bath.

Avoid keeping meat in the water bath for longer than 72 hours

To avoid food safety issues, you should not cook meat sous vide for longer than three days. Botulism can easily develop in food that has been kept in a vacuum for too long since the bacteria which produces it needs an environment without air to grow. In addition, you should eat it as soon as possible after cooking.

Longer is not necessarily better

Although sous vide cooking is more forgiving in terms of the timing, you should still not keep food in the water bath for too long after the recommended time. The longer you keep meat in the sous vide bath, the more moisture it loses. Thus, no matter how long the recommended cooking time, a good rule of thumb to follow is that the meat should not be cooked longer than 36 hours.

If you are ready to cook sous vide seriously, here are some simple recipes that can get you started. Remember to read the recipe thoroughly before starting out, and prepare all the ingredients necessary before you begin cooking.

However, you should not hesitate to adjust quantities of ingredients based on your requirements, since these will not affect cooking times and temperatures too much. Once you've completed the recipe once, you can start experimenting by substituting some ingredients based on your preferences, in order to make a dish that is uniquely your own.

9 - Recipes

Sous Vide Pork Chops

One disadvantage of trying to eat healthier by using leaner cuts of pork is that these tend to dry out more quickly at high temperatures. Cooking them sous vide solves this problem since they are cooked at a lower temperature, resulting in juicier pork that is thoroughly cooked.

Depending on the level of doneness you want, you can set the temperature to 130-degrees F (rare), 140-degrees F (medium-rare), 150-degrees F (medium-well) and 160-degrees F (well done). Make sure the water has reached this final temperature before you place the pork chops in it.

If you are planning to cook the chops at once, generously season them using salt and pepper. If you are planning to leave them in the bag for more than a few hours before you cook them, season them only before you sear them after cooking.

To ensure that the juices of the pork will not get on the edge of the bag and interfere with the integrity of the seal, form a hem by folding the top back over itself. Slide the chops into a bag in one layer. Make sure that the bag is not too full; you can use several bags if necessary. Most of the air in the bag should be removed when sealing and the bag should sink when placed in the water.

Cooking time is determined by the thickness of the chops. For every half-inch thickness, allow fifteen minutes cooking time plus another ten as a margin of error.

Thus, if you have a steak that is 1-1/2 inches thick, you should cook it for at least an hour but no more than 4 hours; if you have thicker chops, then add another fifteen minutes per half-inch thickness. Don't let the pork stay in the water longer than four hours since the meat will become too tender and mushy.

After the pork is removed from the water, dry thoroughly with paper towels or kitchen towels. Place a skillet on the stove over high heat and then add one tablespoon of canola or vegetable oil and one tablespoon of butter. Swirl the pan until the butter starts to brown and is melting.

Put the pork on the skillet and cook for 45 seconds until crust is very crisp and deep brown. Flip and cook on the other side. Once they are browned, pick up the chops with tongs and brown the edges.

Place the chops on a rack set over a baking sheet for a couple of minutes and then serve. If you are not going to serve the chops at once, you can reheat the drippings until they sizzle, and then pour them over the chops to make the crust crisp again.

Sous Vide Fried Chicken Wings

This fried chicken recipe is healthier than traditional ones since it ensures that the wings are thoroughly cooked before they are fried, and you only have to fry them for a shorter time. This recipe is intended to serve four people but you can adjust it for greater or lesser servings.

Ingredients:

- Chicken wings, 8 pieces (dark or light meat)

- Soymilk, 2 cups

- Lemon juice or vinegar, one tablespoon

- Plain flour, one cup

- Rice flour, one cup

- Cornstarch or corn flour, half-cup

- Paprika, 2 tablespoons

- Salt 2 tablespoons

- Ground black pepper, 2 tablespoons

Procedure:

1. Heat water to a final temperature of 154.4-degrees F.

2. Season chicken with salt and pepper then bag it.

3. If dark meat, cook for 3 hours; if light, one hour.

Finishing

1. Remove chicken from water, dry thoroughly and set aside for fifteen to twenty minutes.

2. Preheat the oil in the fryer to 400-degrees F to 425-degrees F.

3. In a bowl, whisk together soy milk and vinegar or

lemon juice. In another bowl, whisk together the dry ingredients.

4. Dredge the chicken in the dry and then the wet mixture. Repeat two to three times then place wings on a wire rack.

5. Deep fry chicken in batches of 2 to 3 pieces for three to four minutes. Set the fried pieces on a wire rack and let cool for fifteen to twenty minutes before serving.

Sous Vide Soft Poached Eggs

Eggs are among the easiest foods to cook sous vide since you don't even need a sous vide machine or a circulator. In this recipe we will include instructions on how you can cook poached eggs using only a large cooler; you can cook up to twelve eggs.

Procedure:

1. If you have a circulator or sous vide machine, set the temperature to 143-degrees F. If you are using a cooler, fill it with hot water; boil water in a kettle and

pour it into the cooler to raise the temperature to 146-degrees F.

2. Place the eggs in the water bath and cook for forty-five minutes. Remove eggs from water and let cool for a while.

3. Fill a medium pot with water and bring it to a bare simmer; then lower the heat until the water stops bubbling entirely.

4. Take one egg and gently crack it at the fat end; peel off a square opening around 1-1/2 inches. Invert egg over a small bowl and let slip out of the opening; if it has been cooked properly it will slip right out of the shell. Repeat with remaining eggs, using a separate bowl for each egg.

5. Carefully pick up eggs one at a time with a perforated spoon; dump excess whites and return eggs to bowls.

6. After all the eggs have been drained, slip them into the pot. Swirl the water occasionally so eggs won't stick to the bottom.

7. Cook for around a minute or until the white outside is just set. Use a perforated spoon to pick up eggs and serve immediately.

8. You can also keep the eggs in the refrigerator for as long as three days; just immerse them in cold water in a sealed container. Reheat eggs by placing them in a bowl with hot water for a few minutes.

Sous Vide Soft Boiled Eggs

You can also use a similar method to cook soft-boiled eggs. This recipe uses an ice bath to stop the cooking process and prepare the eggs for sous vide.

Procedure:

1. If you have a circulator or sous vide machine, set the temperature to 143-degrees F. If you are using a cooler, fill it with hot water; boil water in a kettle and pour it into the cooler to raise the temperature to 146-degrees F.

2. Prepare an ice bath by taking a metal container and filling it with cold water and ice.

3. Fill a large pot with water and bring it to high heat. Place eggs in a strainer or mesh spider and cook for precisely three minutes.

4. Transfer eggs immediately to the ice bath and let chill for a minute.

5. Let eggs cook in sous vide cooker or cooler for forty-five minutes.

6. Serve immediately.

7. You can also store the eggs in the refrigerator for up to three days. To reheat, simply set your sous vide cooker to 135-degrees F and cook the eggs for thirty minutes before serving.

Sous Vide Burgers

Cooking burger patties sous vide allows you to spend less time grilling, and more time socializing with your friends and family. Once the patties come out of the water bath, they are ready to be seared to perfection on the grill.

Ingredients:

- Ground beef, 900 g (20% fat if possible)

- Egg, one large piece (around 50 g)

- Salt

- Black pepper

Procedure:

1. If you have a meat grinder, it is highly recommended that you grind your own beef; otherwise, go for freshly ground beef at the butcher's. Avoid frozen ground beef as much as possible, since it may no longer be fresh and give you the best results.

2. Set the water bath to 133-degrees F.

3. Put the ground beef in the bowl and add the egg; mix until egg is completely incorporated.

4. Portion beef into patties at least 200 g each. Shape patties by forming meat into a ball to remove air and then flattening it. Pinch the sides into shape using your thumbs.

5. Season beef with salt and black pepper before putting into gallon-size Ziploc bags; limit to two per bag to avoid overcrowding.

6. Cook for fifteen to thirty minutes depending on the thickness of the patty. However, it is all right if you leave them there for as long as an hour but do not exceed this time.

7. Place patties on the hot grill, sear for fifteen seconds. Flip and add cheese if desired, then cook for another thirty seconds. If cheese is added, cook an additional fifteen seconds to melt.

Sous Vide Thin-Cut Fries

By pre-cooking the potatoes sous vide before frying them, you get fries that are crispy on the outside and fluffy and light on the inside. The secret is in the three-cooking process, in which the potatoes are cooked sous vide in brine to ensure that the outer crust is a deeper golden brown by slightly elevating its pH.

Ingredients:

- Russet potatoes, Burbank, around a half-kilogram or three unpeeled large potatoes

- Oil for cooking

Brine:

- Water, 1 kg

- Salt, 15 kg

- Glucose syrup, DE 42, 10 g (if not available, you can use 2.5 g of granulated sugar instead)

- Baking soda, 2.5 g

For seasoning:

- Kosher salt and black pepper, ground fine

Procedure:

1. Start by selecting potatoes ideal for frying. Make two bowls of brine with 1 kg water each, one with 90 kg salt and the other with 120 kg. Place potatoes in weaker brine; set aside those that float since they are

too wet to fry. Place potatoes that float into the stronger brine; use those that float for your fries.

2. Peel the potatoes and submerge in water to retard browning.

3. Cut the potatoes into thin fries of around 9 mm each; return to water to prevent browning.

4. Mix ingredients to make brine.

5. Package fries in a bag with around the same weight of fries (to make them easier to handle, use 500 g of fries per bag). Make sure that the fries are in a single layer.

6. Cook the fries for around fifteen minutes until very tender. For best results, cook until the potatoes are almost falling apart.

7. Place fries on a wire rack to cool, making sure they don't touch each other.

8. Fill a large pot around halfway with cooking oil and heat until it reaches 266-degrees F.

9. Lower the fries in small batches into the oil using a slotted spoon or strainer. Cook for around five minutes; the fries should feel firm and dry when removed from the oil.

10. Lay the cooked fries on a wire rack to dry. If not serving at once, the fries can be stored for several months in the freezer; if possible, vacuum pack them before freezing to avoid becoming rancid.

11. If you are going to serve the fries, fill a large pot with oil and heat to 374-degrees F. Make sure that the pot is big enough that the oil will not overflow when you add the fries and there is enough oil that the temperature does not fall too far when cold fries are put in.

12. Fry again until the surface turns golden brown and the bubbles streaming from the cooking slow to a trickle, around a minute and 45 seconds.

13. Drain on paper towels to remove excess oil from fries and prevent them from being greasy.

14. Season to taste with kosher salt and black pepper. Serve. You can also serve the fries with your favorite

dip.

Sous Vide Korean Pork Ribs

If you are feeling adventurous, you might want to try this delicious pork ribs recipe from South Korea. It uses sweet and spicy Hoisin sauce in the glaze to give it a distinctive taste. This recipe serves two to three.

Ingredients:

- Back Ribs, one rack

Marinade:

- Soy Sauce, 120 ml (half-cup)

- Hoisin Sauce, 80 ml (1/3-cup)

- Brown sugar, 50 g (1/4-cup)

- Sesame oil, 30 ml (two tablespoons)

- Peeled and minced garlic cloves, 4 pieces

- Peeled and grated fresh ginger, half-inch piece

- Sriracha sauce, 15 ml to 30 ml, one to two table-spoons

Garnish

- Toasted sesame seeds, 30 g (three tablespoons)

- Sliced and trimmed green onions, six bulbs

Procedure:

1. Peel off the thin membrane from the back of the ribs. Cut into individual portions.

2. Whisk all the marinade ingredients together in a bowl.

3. Place ribs in a Ziploc bag or bowl and add marinade. Toss ribs until they are completely coated in marinade. Refrigerate for around 2 – 3 hours. At around the hour – 90 minute mark, turn ribs over to ensure to ensure both sides are equally coated. Set aside around a half-cup of the marinade.

4. Preheat water to 160-degrees F.

5. Transfer ribs to cooking pouches, around five at a time or just enough per bag that they are only one layer deep. Vacuum seal the bags.

6. Place bags in the water and let cook for eighteen hours.

7. About a half-hour before the ribs are done, make the glaze by cooking the remaining marinade in a saucepan and heating at medium/low heat; reduce heat by half to finish glaze.

8. Before ribs are done, preheat oven to 425-degrees F.

9. Remove pouches from the water and move ribs to a broiling pan using tongs.

10. Brush the ribs with glaze and cook in the oven for five minutes; repeat once more.

11. Serve with a garnish of green onions and sesame seeds.

Sous Vide Glazed Carrots

Carrot lovers will go crazy for this recipe, which produces

tenderized carrots with an intense natural flavor that is enhanced by a sweet delicious glaze. This recipe produces four to six servings.

Ingredients

- Whole baby carrots, well-scrubbed or peeled, 1 pound/Medium to large carrots, one pound, peeled and cut into one-inch pieces

- Unsalted butter, 30g (two tablespoons)

- Granulated sugar, 12g (one tablespoon)

- Kosher salt

- Black pepper, freshly ground

- Chopped parsley, 15ml (one tablespoon) (optional)

Procedure

1. Preheat cooker to 183-degrees F.

2. Place ingredients and half-teaspoon of kosher salt in a vacuum bag and seal.

3. Cook for around an hour or until carrots are fully tender.

4. Empty bag into a heavy bottomed 12-inch skillet. Cook mixture over high heat for around two minutes, stirring constantly until the liquid has turned to a shiny glaze.

5. Season with salt and pepper; add parsley if desired and serve immediately.

6. If the glaze breaks and becomes greasy, re-form glaze by adding a teaspoon of water at a time and then shaking the pan.

7. If you are not planning to cook carrots at once, they can be stored for up to a week in the refrigerator.

Sous Vide Smoky Pulled Pork Shoulder

This recipe will allow you to cook pork so tender you can literally pull it apart with your fingers. The main disadvantage is that it will take a long lead-time to cook, but the results will be more than worth the wait.

Ingredients:

- Pork butt (shoulder), bone-in or boneless, one piece of around five to seven pounds (2.25 kg to 3.25 kg)

- Kosher salt

- Liquid smoke, 3ml (half-teaspoon)

Spice Rub:

- Paprika, 50g (One-fourth cup)

- Dark brown sugar, 50g (one-fourth cup)

- Kosher salt, 35g (three tablespoons)

- Whole yellow mustard seed, 12g (one tablespoon)

- Freshly-ground black pepper, 4g (one teaspoon)

- Granulated garlic powder, 20g (two tablespoons)

- Dried oregano, 8g (one tablespoon)

- Whole coriander seed, 12g (one tablespoon)

- Red pepper flakes, 4g (one teaspoon)

Procedure:

1. Combine spice rub ingredients in a spice grinder in batches; grind to a fine powder.

2. Divide spice rub mixture in half; set aside one of the halves. Rub the mixture into the pork, pressing it firmly until it sticks.

3. Place pork in bag; add liquid smoke if desired; seal.

4. Set cooker at the desired temperature based on the level of doneness desired: if tender but sliceable, 145-degrees F, if traditional texture pulled pork, 165-degrees F.

5. Place bag in a water bath and cook for eighteen to twenty-four hours.

6. If finishing in the oven, set the temperature to 300-degrees F and place rack in middle position. Blot pork dry with paper towels then rub remaining spice mixture on the surface. Prepare wire rack by setting

in a rimmed baking sheet; place pork on it and then put into the oven. Roast for around ninety minutes or until a dark, deep bark has formed.

7. If finishing on a grill, start by lighting half a chimney with charcoal; pour out when all the coals have been lit and are covered with grey ash. Arrange coal on one side of the grill, and then place grate in place then cover grill; preheat for five minutes. Prepare pork as described in step 6 and then place pork on the grill's cooler side. Add four to five chunks of hardwood to the hotter side of grill; cover grill and let pork smoke. Make sure the temperature is maintained at a range of 275-degrees F to 300-degrees F by adjusting vents; while cooking add 2 to 3 chunks twice. Smoke for around 90 minutes or until a bark has formed.

8. Transfer pork to bowl or cutting board. Depending on the level of doneness, shred pork with two forks or slice with a knife into bite-sized pieces. Serve immediately with your favorite barbecue sauce.

9. If pork will not be cooked at once, it can be kept in the refrigerator for as long as a week after sous vide.

Sous Vide Spanish-Style Paprika Shrimp

There are a number of advantages to cooking shrimp sous vide including being able to infuse them with flavor while they are cooking and getting textures that you wouldn't be able to get with traditional cooking methods.

This recipe gives you shrimp infused with Mediterranean flavors including spicy paprika, garlic, and extra-virgin coconut oil. Another trick to cooking shrimp sous vide is tossing it with baking soda to give it a firmer texture.

Depending on the texture you want, there are four cooking temperatures you can choose:

- Semi-raw and translucent, with a buttery, soft texture – 125-degrees F

- Very tender and almost opaque, with a touch of firmness – 130-degrees F

- Tender, juicy and moist, and scarcely opaque - 135-degrees F

- Conventional poached texture, with juicy, crisp bite

and good bounce – 140-degrees F

Ingredients:

- Large shrimp, peeled, 1 ½-pound (700 g)

- Baking soda, half-teaspoon

- Kosher salt

- Extra-virgin olive oil, 90 ml (six tablespoons)

- Garlic, six thinly sliced medium cloves

- Spanish paprika, 6 g (one tablespoon)

- Sherry, 45 ml (three tablespoons)

- Bay leaves, two pieces

- Butter, 30 g (two tablespoons)

- Sherry vinegar, 6 ml (1 ½-tablespoons)

Procedure:

1. Set sous vide cooker temperature based on the de-

sired texture.

2. Toss shrimp in a large bowl with baking soda and half-teaspoon kosher salt; set aside.

3. Heat the garlic and olive oil over medium heat in a large skillet. Cook for around three minutes, constantly stirring, until garlic sizzles and softens but does not turn brown. Add bay leaves and paprika, cook for another thirty seconds, constantly stirring until it becomes fragrant. Then add the sherry and sherry vinegar, and cook at high for around two minutes, until the sauce begins to emulsify and the liquid is reduced. Remove skillet from heat and stir in butter. Season with salt to taste and let cool for around five minutes.

4. Place shrimp in the vacuum bag or heavy-duty sealer bag; pour in garlic/olive oil mixture and then remove all the air using displacement method or vacuum sealer. Press bag so shrimp are arranged in a single layer.

5. Place bag in a water bath and cook for at least fifteen

minutes but no more than an hour.

6. Pour shrimp into a warmed bowl and serve with crusty bread for sopping up excess sauce.

Sous Vide Poached Shrimp

Here's a recipe for traditional poached shrimp with a sous vide twist: not only will you enjoy more flavorful shrimp, you can infuse it with butter while cooking to add extra flavor.

Cooking temperature chart:

- Semi-raw and translucent, with a buttery, soft texture – 125-degrees F

- Very tender and almost opaque, with a touch of firmness – 130-degrees F

- Tender, juicy and moist, and scarcely opaque - 135-degrees F

- Conventional poached texture, with juicy, crisp bite and good bounce – 140-degrees F

Ingredients:

- Large shrimp, peeled, 1 ½-pound (700 g)

- Baking soda, half-teaspoon

- Kosher salt

- Extra-virgin olive oil or butter (optional)

- Aromatics such as garlic, parsley or shallots (optional)

Procedure:

1. Use temperature chart to choose the cooking temperature. Set water bath to the desired temperature.

2. In a large bowl, toss shrimp with kosher salt and baking soda. Place in a heavy-duty Ziploc bag or vacuum bag; if desired add butter or olive oil and aromatics.

3. Cook for a minimum of fifteen minutes to no more than an hour.

4. Serve at once or chill first then serve cold.

Sous Vide Steaks

Cooking steaks sous vide gives you perfectly even results through slow cooking that you can replicate every time. After cooking, you can finish the steaks on a grill or pan to give it a dark crust.

Temperature Cooking Chart:

Butcher's Cut/Tenderloin/T-Bone/Porterhouse/Strip

- Very Rare to Rare – 120-degrees F to 128-degrees F – one hour to 2 ½-hours

- Medium Rare – 129-degrees F to 134-degrees F – one hour to four hours (or no more than 2 ½-hours if cooked at less than 130-degrees F)

- Medium – 135-degrees F to 144-degrees F - one to four hours

- Medium-well – 145-degrees F to 155-degrees F – one hour to 3 ½-hours

- Well Done – 156-degrees F and up – one hour to

three hours

Tenderloin

- Very Rare to Rare – 120-degrees F to 128-degrees F – 45 minutes to 2 ½-hours

- Medium Rare – 129-degrees F to 134-degrees F – 45 minutes to four hours (or no more than 2 ½-hours if cooked at less than 130-degrees F)

- Medium – 135-degrees F to 144-degrees F – 45 minutes to four hours

- Medium-well – 145-degrees F to 155-degrees F – 45 minutes to 3 ½-hours

- Well Done – 156-degrees F and up – one hour to three hours

Ingredients:

- Steaks, two (1 ½-inch to 2 inch thick) pieces (porterhouse, T-bone, strip or ribeye) or four (6 to 8 oz.) pieces tenderloin

- Freshly ground black pepper and kosher salt

- Canola oil, two tablespoons

- Butter, two tablespoons

- Rosemary or thyme, two sprigs (optional)

- Garlic, two cloves (optional)

- Shallots, two pieces, thinly sliced (optional)

Procedure:

1. Preheat sous vide cooker to the desired temperature. Season steaks with salt and pepper and place in bag with spices if desired. Seal bags then place in water bath for appropriate cooking time. Pat dry thoroughly before cooking.

2. If using a pan to finish, open your windows first since cooking will produce smoke. Place canola, rice bran or vegetable oil in a stainless steel or cast iron skillet and put on the hottest burner; preheat until oil starts to smoke. Put the steak in the skillet (if desired, add one tablespoon butter or omit to get a cleaner-tasting

sear), and then cook one side for fifteen to thirty seconds and then flip and cook for fifteen to thirty seconds. Keep flipping the steak for around ninety seconds until the desired sear is achieved. If you did not add butter earlier, you can do so thirty seconds before steak is done. Serve immediately.

3. If you are using a charcoal grill, take a chimney full of charcoal and light it; when all the charcoal is covered in a light grey ash arrange the coals on one side of the grate. If using gas-fired grill then set half the burners to the highest setting, and then cover and preheat for ten minutes.

4. Place cooking grate, cover grill and preheat for five minutes. Clean and oil the grate then place steak on the hot side. Cook steak for around ninety seconds, turning it over every fifteen to thirty seconds until rich, deep crust has formed. If the fire flares up due to dripping fat, transfer steak to cooler side or suffocate fire by closing lid until it dies out.

5. Transfer steak to serving platter or cutting board and serve immediately.

Sous Vide Yoghurt

The main advantage of using sous vide to make yogurt is that you can greatly shorten the process from several days to just a few hours. It yields around five servings. However, you will need cooking jars rather than sealable bags.

Ingredients:

- Whole milk, 800 g

- Live culture yogurt, 40 g

Procedure:

1. Preheat sous vide cooker to 109-degrees F.

2. In a pot warm milk to 180-degrees F over low heat. While heating, run a spatula around the bottom to ensure the milk doesn't scald. Remove from heat and cool down; alternatively, you can prepare an ice bath to cool down the milk more quickly. The final temperature of the milk should be 110-degrees F.

3. Place live culture yogurt in a bowl with a spoon. Add

some of the milk and then stir until smooth. Add the remaining milk and then stir mixture until fully combined.

4. Pour mixture into a one-liter jar or several smaller jars. Screw lids on tightly.

5. Transfer jars to the water bath. Let stay for at least five hours.

6. Remove jars from water and transfer to refrigerator. Let sit overnight before eating.

Sous Vide Crème Brule

One of the biggest challenges in preparing Crème Brule using traditional methods is that there is a risk it will curdle if the internal temperature goes above 185-degrees F. Sous vide avoids this problem by cooking the custards at a precise temperature.

To add that delicious final touch, a blowtorch is used to create a layer of golden-brown caramelized sugar before serving. You will need canning jars instead of sealable packages for this recipe.

Ingredients:

- Egg yolks, eleven or around 160 g

- Granulated sugar, 90 g

- Heavy cream, 600 g

- Salt, 3 g

Procedure:

1. Preheat sous vide cooker to 176-degrees F.

2. In a bowl, combine egg yolks, salt, and sugar; whisk mixture until smooth.

3. If desired, heat cream in a pot to 158-degrees F (optional); otherwise, pour cream into egg yolk mixture. Introduce the cream slowly to avoid curdling, then gradually increase pour rate.

4. Strain mixture using a fine mesh strainer. Let rest for around a half-hour to allow bubbles to dissipate. Any remaining bubbles on the surface can be skimmed away.

5. Place some 150 g of custard mixture per jar; avoid pouring too quickly or from too high a level so bubbles won't form on the surface.

6. Just barely close the lids in such a way that you can still open them with your fingertips. This is important since it allows air to escape from the jars. If the lid is closed too tight, the air pressure inside the jar may cause it to crack.

7. Place jars in water bath and cook for an hour.

8. Remove from water and let rest at room temperature.

9. Prepare an ice bath, then transfer the jars to it and chill. Once the jars are cold, tighten the lids and transfer to refrigerator. The Crème Brule will last for around a week.

To create caramelized top layer:

1. Open the jar; if condensation has formed on top of the custard, remove by dabbing with the corner of a paper towel.

2. Dust a layer of granulated sugar on top using your fingers or a small sieve; the more sugar, the more crunchy and caramelized the layer will be.

3. Turn the blowtorch on at low-gas release. Hold the torch in your dominant hand and the jar in the other; aim the flame at the custard while rotating the jar with your hand. Move the torch closer and farther to control the heat; the distance between the torch and the jar should range from 10 inches to 24 inches.

4. When the layer has turned the desired color, let the sugar set for five minutes before eating to allow it to achieve maximum crunchiness.

Sous Vide Lemon Curd

This recipe cooks the ingredients sous vide to create an oozy, soft curd.

Ingredients:

- Lemons, four pieces

- Butter, 200 g

- Sugar, 175 g (dextrose can also be used)

- Egg yolks, eight pieces or around 120 g

- Citric acid, 5 g

- Salt, 1 g

- 180-bloom gelatin, 13 g (optional)

- Ice water

Procedure:

1. Preheat water to 167-degrees F.

2. Use lemons to create 10 g of zest and 150 g of lemon juice (if you don't know how to make zest, see instructions below).

3. Combine ingredients along with lemon zest in a small Ziploc bag or sous vide pouch. If you would like it to be less sweet, you can replace it with dextrose. You can also add gelatin if you want the curd to have a texture that is more jam-like.

4. Cook for one hour.

5. Transfer curd to a blender and blend on high for thirty to sixty seconds, until the mixture is fully emulsified. You should stop blending when the curd stops changing color, since as you blend the color will lighten.

6. If there are air bubbles, you can remove them by transferring the curd to chamber sealer or knock the bowl on the counter several times.

7. To chill, transfer the curd to bowl and place in ice bath.

To make lemon zest:

1. With a paring knife, cut strips of zest from the skin of the lemon but make sure that you avoid too much pith; leaving too much pit can cause the zest to taste bitter. You can do this by cutting the top and bottom of the lemon so you can see where the pith is.

2. Place the knife on the edge of the skin. Guide the knife down following the curve of the skin. Chop it

finely to use in the recipe above or you can leave it in strips for other uses.

3. If you have a grater, you can create zest by lightly grazing the skin, either moving in a circular motion or in strips.

Sous Vide Crispy Chicken with Cheddar Broccoli Sauce

This delicious dish will surely be a staple in your household once you've tried it.

Ingredients:

- Chicken legs, 4 pieces, skin-on

- Broccoli Cheddar Sauce:

- Broccoli, one whole head

- Sweet onion, half piece, medium diced

- Unsalted butter, 40 g

- Salt, 5 g

- Minced garlic, 4 g

- White wine, 82 g

- Heavy cream, 340 g

- Aged white cheddar, 100 g

- Black pepper to taste

- White button mushrooms, six pieces cut into quarters (optional)

Procedure:

To make the sauce:

1. Trim off broccoli florets with a paring knife; set aside. Chop remainder roughly.

2. Combine chopped broccoli stems and leavings with onion in food processor and pulse until mixture is finely minced.

3. Place butter, garlic, and salt along with onion-broccoli mixture in a pot and cook slowly over medium-

high heat. Let sweat until garlic and onions have cooked down and are fragrant, around six minutes.

4. Add white wine and reduce; when almost no clear liquid is left, add cheese and cream. Reduce until it has achieved a fondue-like consistency; avoid scorching by whisking frequently (for this recipe, however, it should only be reduced halfway). Let sit until you are ready to serve.

5. Heat sauce and reduce until it has reached a thick consistency.

6. Add the broccoli florets and mushrooms (optional); reduce heat to low. Cover.

7. Season with black pepper

To make chicken:

1. Heat water to 158-degrees F.

2. Place chicken legs in Ziploc bag with some oil.

3. Immerse in water and cook for around an hour.

4. Thoroughly pat dry using paper towels.

5. Generously add enough oil to a cast-iron skillet or non-stick pan to ensure it is covered. Heat until the oil starts to smoke and then put thighs in a pan with skin side down using tongs.

6. Sear for around a minute, until skin is golden brown. Season with salt to taste.

7. To serve, place a mound of the sauce onto plate or bowl, and lightly drizzle with extra-virgin olive oil.

8. Place a thigh on top of sauce; if desired, garnish with flat leaf parsley.

9. If desired, you can serve on preheated dishes. Simply place the serving dishes in an oven that has been set to lowest setting; remove when ready to serve.

10 - Conclusion

Thank you for buying this book!

I hope that this book was useful in helping you learn to cook sous vide. Although this cooking technique may seem odd at first, once you've gotten used to preparing food this way, you'll realize how easy it actually is and how much better food made this way tastes.

Thank you again and good luck!

Thank You

As we reach the end of this book, I want to say thanks for reading this book.

I want to get this information out to as many people as possible. If you found this book helpful, I would greatly appreciate you leaving me a review. This helps others find the book as well.

Disclaimer

This document is geared towards providing exact and reliable information in regards to the topic and issue covered. The publication is sold on the idea that the publisher is not required to render an accounting, officially permitted, or otherwise, qualified services. If advice is necessary, legal, financial, medical or professional, a practiced individual in the profession should be ordered.

This information is not presented by a financial or medical practitioner and is for entertainment, educational and informational purposes only. The content is not intended as a substitute for professional medical advice, diagnosis, or treatment. Always seek the advice of your physician or other qualified health care provider with any questions you may have regarding a medical condition. Never disregard professional medical advice or delay in seeking it because of something you have read.

The information provided herein is stated to be truthful and consistent, in that any liability, in terms of inattention or otherwise, by any usage or abuse of any policies, processes, or directions contained within is the solitary and utter responsibility of the recipient reader. Under no circumstances